Table Of Contents

Chapter 1: Introduction to New Orleans Cuisine

The History of New Orleans Cuisine

New Orleans cuisine is a melting pot of flavors and influences, reflecting the city's rich and diverse history. The city's culinary traditions can be traced back to its founding in 1718 by French colonists, who brought with them a love of rich sauces, buttery pastries, and decadent desserts.

Over the years, New Orleans cuisine has been shaped by waves of immigrants, including Spanish, African, and Italian settlers, as well as the indigenous Choctaw and Houma tribes. Each group brought their own culinary traditions and ingredients, leading to the unique blend of flavors that define New Orleans cuisine today.

One of the most iconic dishes to come out of this culinary fusion is gumbo, a hearty stew made with a roux base, okra, and a variety of meats and seafood.

Gumbo is a staple in New Orleans homes and restaurants, and is considered a symbol of the city's multicultural heritage.

Another beloved dish is jambalaya, a rice-based dish that can be made with a variety of meats, seafood, and vegetables. Jambalaya is a favorite at family gatherings, festivals, and celebrations, and is a true representation of the city's vibrant and diverse food culture.

New Orleans is also known for its sweet treats, including beignets and king cake. Beignets are fluffy, powdered sugar-coated pastries that are typically enjoyed with a hot cup of coffee. King cake is a Mardi Gras tradition, a sweet and colorful pastry enjoyed during the carnival season.

Overall, New Orleans cuisine is a celebration of flavors, traditions, and history. Whether you're craving a hearty bowl of gumbo, a spicy plate of jambalaya, or a sweet and indulgent king cake, the city's culinary offerings are sure to satisfy your taste buds and leave you craving more.

The Influence of Cajun and Creole Cuisine

One of the most distinctive aspects of New Orleans cuisine is the influence of Cajun and Creole cooking styles. While both cuisines have their own unique flavors and ingredients, they share a common love for bold and flavorful dishes that are sure to tantalize your taste buds.

Cajun cuisine, which hails from the Acadian settlers of Louisiana, is characterized by its use of bold spices and hearty ingredients such as Andouille sausage, bell peppers, and onions. Dishes like gumbo, jambalaya, and red beans and rice are staples of Cajun cooking and are beloved by locals and visitors alike.

On the other hand, Creole cuisine, which has its roots in the French, Spanish, African, and Native American influences of New Orleans, is known for its more refined and complex flavors. Creole dishes often feature a combination of fresh seafood, tomatoes, and a variety of herbs and spices. Classics like shrimp etouffee, crawfish bisque, and bananas foster are all examples of Creole culinary delights.

The fusion of these two distinct culinary traditions has created a melting pot of flavors that is uniquely New Orleans. Whether you're craving a spicy bowl of gumbo or a decadent slice of king cake, Cajun and Creole cuisine has something to offer for everyone.

So, the next time you find yourself outside of New Orleans, be sure to bring a taste of the Big Easy into your own kitchen with some easy-to-make recipes inspired by the rich culinary heritage of Cajun and Creole cooking. Your taste buds will thank you!

Common Ingredients in New Orleans Recipes

If you're a fan of New Orleans cuisine but aren't quite sure where to start when it comes to cooking up some classic dishes, understanding the common ingredients used in these recipes is a great place to begin. New Orleans cuisine is known for its bold flavors, unique spices, and a fusion of influences from French, Spanish, African, and Native American cultures.

One common ingredient you'll find in many New Orleans recipes is the "holy trinity" of onions, bell peppers, and celery. This trio forms the base of many dishes, providing a savory and aromatic foundation for flavors to build upon. Another staple in New Orleans cooking is roux, a mixture of flour and fat that is cooked until it reaches a deep, rich brown color. Roux is used as a thickening agent in many New Orleans dishes, including gumbo and étouffée.

Seafood is another key component of many New Orleans recipes, thanks to the city's proximity to the Gulf of Mexico. Shrimp, crab, oysters, and crawfish are all commonly used in dishes like jambalaya, seafood gumbo, and shrimp étouffée. And let's not forget about the spices! New Orleans cuisine is known for its bold flavors, thanks to a mix of spices like cayenne pepper, paprika, thyme, and bay leaves.

Whether you're looking to whip up a traditional gumbo or try your hand at making beignets, understanding the common ingredients used in New Orleans recipes will help you capture the essence of this vibrant cuisine. So grab your apron and get ready to bring a taste of the Big Easy to your kitchen!

Chapter 2: Classic New Orleans Recipes

Shrimp Etouffee

Shrimp Etouffee is a classic Creole dish that is sure to transport your taste buds straight to the vibrant streets of New Orleans. This flavorful and comforting dish is a staple in Louisiana cuisine, and is perfect for any occasion, whether you're hosting a Mardi Gras party or simply craving some authentic Southern comfort food.

Ingredients:

For the Shrimp Stock:

- Shrimp shells and heads (reserved from peeled shrimp)
- 4 cups water
- 1 onion, quartered
- 2 celery stalks, chopped
- 2 garlic cloves, smashed
- 1 bay leaf
- 1 teaspoon black peppercorns
- Salt, to taste

For the Etouffee:

- 1/2 cup vegetable oil or butter
- 1/2 cup all-purpose flour
- 1 onion, diced
- 1 green bell pepper, diced
- 2 celery stalks, diced
- 3 cloves garlic, minced
- 1 can (14.5 ounces) diced tomatoes
- 1 teaspoon paprika
- 1/2 teaspoon cayenne pepper (adjust to taste)
- 1/2 teaspoon dried thyme
- 1/2 teaspoon dried oregano
- 2 cups shrimp stock (strained)
- 1 pound shrimp, peeled and deveined
- Salt and black pepper, to taste
- Cooked rice, for serving
- Chopped green onions, for garnish

Instructions:

1. Prepare the Shrimp Stock:

- In a large pot, combine the shrimp shells and heads (reserved from peeled shrimp) with water, onion, celery, garlic, bay leaf, black peppercorns, and salt.

- Once the stock has simmered and developed flavor, strain it through a fine mesh sieve or cheesecloth to remove the solids. Set the shrimp stock aside for later use.

2. Make the Etouffee:

- In a large skillet or Dutch oven, heat the vegetable oil or butter over medium heat. Once hot, add the flour to make a roux.
- Cook the roux, stirring constantly, until it reaches a dark caramel color, similar to peanut butter. Be careful not to burn it.
- Add the diced onion, bell pepper, and celery to the roux. Cook, stirring occasionally, until the vegetables are softened, about 5-7 minutes.
- Stir in the minced garlic and cook for an additional 1-2 minutes until fragrant.
- Add the diced tomatoes (with their juices) to the skillet, along with the paprika, cayenne pepper, dried thyme, and dried oregano. Stir to combine.
- Gradually pour in the shrimp stock, stirring constantly to incorporate it into the mixture and prevent lumps from forming.

- Bring the mixture to a simmer and let it cook for about 15-20 minutes, stirring occasionally, to allow the flavors to meld together and the sauce to thicken.

- Once the sauce has thickened to your desired consistency, add the peeled and deveined shrimp to the skillet. Cook the shrimp for 3-5 minutes, or until they turn pink and opaque.

- Season the etouffee with salt and black pepper to taste.

3. Serve:

- Serve the shrimp etouffee hot over cooked rice.
- Garnish each serving with chopped green onions for a pop of freshness and flavor.

Enjoy your homemade New Orleans-style Shrimp Etouffee, packed with rich flavors and Southern charm!

Whether you're a seasoned pro at cooking New Orleans recipes or a novice looking to expand your culinary horizons, Shrimp Etouffee is a must-try dish that will impress your friends and family.

So grab your apron and get ready to experience the flavors of the Big Easy in your own home with this delicious recipe.

Red Beans and Rice

Red beans and rice is a classic Creole dish that has been a staple in New Orleans for generations. This simple yet flavorful meal is a favorite among locals and visitors alike, and it's easy to see why.

Ingredients:

For the Red Beans:

- 1 pound dried red kidney beans
- 1 tablespoon vegetable oil
- 1 large onion, diced
- 1 green bell pepper, diced
- 2 celery stalks, diced
- 4 cloves garlic, minced
- 1 bay leaf
- 1 teaspoon dried thyme
- 1 teaspoon dried oregano
- 1 teaspoon smoked paprika
- 1/2 teaspoon cayenne pepper (adjust to taste)

- 1 pound smoked sausage or Andouille sausage, sliced into rounds
- Salt and black pepper, to taste
- Cooked white rice, for serving
- Chopped green onions, for garnish

Instructions:

1. Prepare the Red Beans:

- Rinse the dried red kidney beans under cold water and remove any debris or stones.

- Drain and rinse the soaked beans before cooking.

2. Cook the Red Beans:

- In a large pot or Dutch oven, heat the vegetable oil over medium heat. Add the diced onion, bell pepper, and celery to the pot. Cook, stirring occasionally, until the vegetables are softened, about 5-7 minutes.

- Add the minced garlic to the pot and cook for an additional 1-2 minutes until fragrant.

- Stir in the soaked red kidney beans, bay leaf, dried thyme, dried oregano, smoked paprika, and cayenne pepper. Pour in enough water to cover the beans by about 2 inches.

- Bring the mixture to a boil, then reduce the heat to low and let it simmer, partially covered, for about 1.5-2 hours, or until the beans are tender and creamy, stirring occasionally.

- During the last 30 minutes of cooking, add the sliced smoked sausage or Andouille sausage to the pot. Let the sausage simmer with the beans until heated through and flavorful.
- Season the red beans with salt and black pepper to taste.

3. Serve:

- Serve the New Orleans-style Red Beans hot over cooked white rice.
- Garnish each serving with chopped green onions for a pop of color and flavor.

Enjoy your homemade New Orleans-style Red Beans and Rice, packed with rich flavors and Southern charm!

Whether you're a fan of New Orleans cuisine or just looking to try something new, red beans and rice is a dish that is sure to become a favorite in your household. So grab a bowl, dig in, and enjoy a taste of the Big Easy right in your own home.

Crawfish Boil

For folks outside of New Orleans, a crawfish boil may seem like a foreign concept. However, in the Big Easy, a crawfish boil is a beloved tradition that brings friends and family together for a day of feasting and fun.

A crawfish boil is a quintessential New Orleans experience that involves cooking up a big pot of spicy crawfish, along with other seafood, vegetables, and spices. The key to a successful crawfish boil is to use fresh ingredients and to season them just right.

Ingredients:

For the Boil:

- 30 pounds live crawfish
- 8 gallons water
- 4 cups kosher salt

- 2 cups Cajun or Creole seasoning
- 2 cups hot sauce (optional)
- 8 lemons, halved
- 6 onions, quartered
- 6 heads garlic, halved crosswise
- 12 bay leaves
- 2 pounds small red potatoes
- 8 ears corn, shucked and halved
- 2 pounds smoked sausage, cut into chunks
- Additional Cajun seasoning, for serving

For Serving:

- Melted butter
- Cocktail sauce
- Remoulade sauce
- Lemon wedges
- Chopped parsley

Instructions:

1. Prepare the Crawfish:

- Rinse the live crawfish under cold water in a large tub or sink. Discard any dead crawfish or debris.

- Purge the crawfish by soaking them in cold, salted water for about 20-30 minutes. This helps to remove any impurities from the crawfish.

2. Set up the Boiling Pot:

Fill a large outdoor boiling pot with 8 gallons of water. Place the pot on a propane burner and bring the water to a rolling boil.

3. Season the Water:

Once the water is boiling, add the kosher salt, Cajun or Creole seasoning, and hot sauce (if using). Stir to dissolve the seasonings into the water.

4. Add Aromatics:

Squeeze the lemon halves into the boiling water and add them to the pot, along with the onion quarters, garlic heads, and bay leaves. Let the aromatics simmer in the seasoned water for about 10 minutes to infuse flavor.

5. Boil the Ingredients:

- Add the red potatoes to the pot and let them cook for about 10 minutes, until they start to soften.

- Next, add the halved ears of corn and chunks of smoked sausage to the pot. Let them cook for an additional 5-7 minutes.

6. Add the Crawfish:

Carefully add the live crawfish to the boiling water. Stir gently to ensure that all the crawfish are submerged in the seasoned water.

7. Boil the Crawfish:

Bring the water back to a boil and let the crawfish boil for about 10-12 minutes, or until they turn bright red and float to the surface of the water.

8. Drain and Serve:

- Once the crawfish are cooked, turn off the heat and carefully drain the boiling pot into a large colander or basket set over a cooler or clean sink.

- Spread out the boiled crawfish, potatoes, corn, and sausage on a large table covered with newspaper or butcher paper.

- Serve the New Orleans-style Crawfish Boil hot, alongside melted butter, cocktail sauce, remoulade sauce, lemon wedges, and chopped parsley. Sprinkle additional Cajun seasoning over the crawfish for extra flavor, if desired.

Enjoy your delicious New Orleans-style Crawfish Boil, and don't forget to grab a cold drink to wash it down!

In New Orleans, a crawfish boil is more than just a meal – it's a social event that brings people together to share good food and good times. So why not bring a taste of the Big Easy to your next gathering with a delicious crawfish boil? Your friends and family are sure to thank you!

Muffuletta Sandwich

If you're a fan of New Orleans cuisine, then you have to try the iconic Muffuletta sandwich. This delicious sandwich is a staple in the Big Easy and is a must-try for anyone looking to experience the flavors of New Orleans.

The Muffuletta sandwich is a unique creation that is packed full of flavor and history. It originated in the Italian immigrant community of New Orleans and quickly became a favorite among locals and visitors alike. The sandwich is made with a round loaf of Italian bread that is filled with layers of deli meats, cheeses, and a tangy olive salad.

Ingredients:

For the Olive Salad:

- 1 cup pitted green olives, chopped
- 1 cup pitted Kalamata olives, chopped
- 1/2 cup giardiniera (pickled vegetable mix), chopped
- 1/4 cup roasted red peppers, chopped
- 2 cloves garlic, minced

- 2 tablespoons capers, chopped
- 1/4 cup chopped fresh parsley
- 1/4 cup extra-virgin olive oil
- 2 tablespoons red wine vinegar
- Salt and pepper to taste

For the Sandwich:

- 1 round loaf of Italian bread or Muffuletta bread
- 4 ounces sliced Genoa salami
- 4 ounces sliced mortadella
- 4 ounces sliced ham
- 4 ounces sliced provolone cheese
- 4 ounces sliced mozzarella cheese

Instructions:

1. Prepare the Olive Salad:

- In a medium bowl, combine the chopped green olives, Kalamata olives, giardiniera, roasted red peppers, garlic, capers, and parsley.

- Drizzle the olive oil and red wine vinegar over the olive mixture.

- Season with salt and pepper to taste.
- Stir the ingredients until well combined.
- Cover the bowl and let the olive salad marinate in the refrigerator for at least 1 hour, or preferably overnight, to allow the flavors to meld.

2. Assemble the Sandwich:

- Slice the loaf of Italian bread or Muffuletta bread horizontally.
- Spread a generous layer of the olive salad on the bottom half of the bread.
- Layer the salami, mortadella, ham, provolone, and mozzarella on top of the olive salad.
- Place the top half of the bread on top of the layers.

3. Serve the Muffuletta:

- Wrap the sandwich tightly in plastic wrap or foil.

- Let the sandwich sit for at least 30 minutes to allow the flavors to meld together.

- When ready to serve, unwrap the sandwich and cut it into wedges.
- Serve the Muffuletta sandwich as a whole or as individual servings.

Enjoy your delicious New Orleans-style Muffuletta Sandwich, packed with flavorful meats, cheeses, and olive salad!

Chapter 3: Seafood Delights

Crawfish Pie

If you've never had the pleasure of trying a delicious Crawfish Pie, then you are truly missing out on a quintessential New Orleans dish. This savory pie is a favorite among locals and visitors alike, with its rich and flavorful filling that is sure to satisfy your taste buds.

Ingredients:

For the Pie Crust:

- 2 1/2 cups all-purpose flour
- 1 teaspoon salt
- 1 cup (2 sticks) unsalted butter, cold and cubed
- 6-8 tablespoons ice water

For the Filling:

- 1 pound peeled crawfish tails
- 1/4 cup unsalted butter
- 1/2 cup diced onion
- 1/2 cup diced bell pepper
- 1/2 cup diced celery
- 2 cloves garlic, minced
- 1/4 cup all-purpose flour
- 1 cup seafood stock or chicken broth
- 1/2 cup heavy cream
- 1 teaspoon Cajun seasoning
- Salt and pepper to taste
- 1/4 cup chopped green onions
- 1/4 cup chopped parsley

Instructions:

1. Prepare the Pie Crust:

- In a large bowl, whisk together the flour and salt.
- Add the cold, cubed butter to the flour mixture.
- Using a pastry cutter or your fingers, work the butter into the flour until the mixture resembles coarse crumbs.

- Gradually add the ice water, 1 tablespoon at a time, mixing until the dough just comes together.
- Divide the dough into two equal portions, shape each portion into a disc, and wrap them in plastic wrap.
- Refrigerate the dough for at least 1 hour before rolling out.

2. Make the Filling:

- In a large skillet, melt the butter over medium heat.
- Add the diced onion, bell pepper, and celery to the skillet. Cook, stirring occasionally, until the vegetables are softened, about 5-7 minutes.

- Add the minced garlic to the skillet and cook for an additional 1-2 minutes until fragrant.

- Stir in the flour and cook for 2-3 minutes to make a roux.

- Gradually whisk in the seafood stock or chicken broth, stirring constantly to prevent lumps from forming.

- Bring the mixture to a simmer and cook until thickened, about 5 minutes.
- Stir in the heavy cream, Cajun seasoning, salt, and pepper.
- Add the peeled crawfish tails to the skillet and cook for 3-4 minutes, or until heated through.
- Remove the skillet from the heat and stir in the chopped green onions and parsley. Set the filling aside to cool slightly.

3. Assemble and Bake the Pie:

- Preheat the oven to 375°F (190°C).
- Roll out one portion of the chilled pie dough on a floured surface to fit a 9-inch pie dish. Place the rolled-out dough into the pie dish and trim any excess dough.

- Pour the crawfish filling into the prepared pie crust.

- Roll out the second portion of pie dough and place it over the filling. Trim any excess dough and crimp the edges to seal the pie.

- Cut a few slits in the top crust to allow steam to escape.

- Optional: Brush the top crust with an egg wash (1 beaten egg mixed with 1 tablespoon of water) for a golden finish.
- Place the pie on a baking sheet to catch any drips, and bake in the preheated oven for 30-35 minutes, or until the crust is golden brown.
- Remove the pie from the oven and let it cool for 10-15 minutes before serving.

Enjoy your delicious New Orleans-style Crawfish Pie, filled with savory crawfish and aromatic vegetables, wrapped in a flaky, buttery crust!

Blackened Catfish

If you're a fan of New Orleans cuisine, then you simply must try the delicious and flavorful dish of Blackened Catfish. This classic Cajun dish is a favorite among locals and visitors alike, and it's easy to see why once you take your first bite.

One of the best things about blackened catfish is that it can be easily made at home, even if you're not in New Orleans.

Simply pick up some fresh catfish fillets from your local seafood market, whip up a batch of Cajun seasoning, and get ready to enjoy a taste of the Big Easy right in your own kitchen.

Ingredients:

For the Blackening Spice Blend:

- 2 tablespoons paprika
- 1 tablespoon garlic powder
- 1 tablespoon onion powder
- 1 tablespoon dried thyme
- 1 tablespoon dried oregano
- 1 teaspoon cayenne pepper
- 1 teaspoon black pepper
- 1 teaspoon salt

For the Catfish:

- 4 catfish fillets (about 6-8 ounces each)
- 1/2 cup unsalted butter, melted
- Lemon wedges, for serving

Instructions:

1. Prepare the Blackening Spice Blend:

In a small bowl, combine the paprika, garlic powder, onion powder, dried thyme, dried oregano, cayenne pepper, black pepper, and salt. Mix well to combine.

2. Coat the Catfish:

- Pat the catfish fillets dry with paper towels.
- Generously coat both sides of each catfish fillet with the blackening spice blend, pressing the seasoning into the fish to adhere.

3. Heat the Skillet:

Heat a cast-iron skillet or heavy-bottomed skillet over high heat until smoking hot.

4. Blacken the Catfish:

- Carefully add about 2 tablespoons of melted butter to the hot skillet.
- Add the seasoned catfish fillets to the skillet, being careful not to overcrowd the pan. You may need to cook the fillets in batches.

- Cook the catfish fillets for 2-3 minutes on each side, or until blackened and cooked through. The fish should easily flake with a fork when done.

- As the catfish cooks, baste the tops with additional melted butter.

5. Serve:

- Transfer the blackened catfish fillets to a serving platter.
- Garnish with lemon wedges.
- Serve the blackened catfish hot, alongside your favorite sides such as rice, vegetables, or coleslaw.

Enjoy your flavorful New Orleans-style Blackened Catfish, packed with aromatic spices and a deliciously crispy crust!

Whether you're looking to impress guests at your next dinner party or simply craving a taste of New Orleans, blackened catfish is the perfect dish to try. So fire up the skillet, grab your Cajun seasoning, and get ready to experience the bold flavors of this classic New Orleans recipe. Trust us, your taste buds will thank you.

Oyster Po'boys

If you've never had the pleasure of sinking your teeth into a delicious Oyster Po'boy, then you are truly missing out on one of the most iconic dishes of New Orleans. This delectable sandwich is a staple in the city's culinary scene, and for good reason - it's absolutely mouthwatering.

Ingredients:

For the Oysters:

- 1 pint fresh oysters, shucked
- 1 cup buttermilk
- 1 cup all-purpose flour
- 1 cup cornmeal
- 1 teaspoon Cajun seasoning
- Vegetable oil, for frying

For the Remoulade Sauce:

- 1/2 cup mayonnaise
- 2 tablespoons Creole mustard or whole grain mustard
- 2 tablespoons chopped pickles or pickle relish
- 1 tablespoon fresh lemon juice
- 1 clove garlic, minced
- 1 teaspoon paprika
- 1/2 teaspoon hot sauce (optional)
- Salt and pepper to taste

For Assembling the Po'boys:

- French baguettes or po'boy rolls, sliced lengthwise
- Shredded lettuce
- Sliced tomatoes
- Sliced dill pickles
- Lemon wedges (for serving)

Instructions:

1. Prepare the Oysters:

- In a medium bowl, soak the shucked oysters in buttermilk for 15-30 minutes.
- In a separate shallow dish, mix together the flour, cornmeal, and Cajun seasoning.
- Remove the oysters from the buttermilk and dredge them in the flour mixture, shaking off any excess.

2. Fry the Oysters:

- In a large skillet or deep fryer, heat vegetable oil to 350°F (175°C).
- Carefully add the breaded oysters to the hot oil in batches, frying for 2-3 minutes or until golden brown and crispy.
- Use a slotted spoon to transfer the fried oysters to a paper towel-lined plate to drain excess oil. Keep warm while you fry the remaining batches.

3. Make the Remoulade Sauce:

In a small bowl, whisk together the mayonnaise, Creole mustard, chopped pickles, lemon juice, minced garlic, paprika, hot sauce (if using), salt, and pepper until well combined. Adjust seasoning to taste.

4. Assemble the Po'boys:

- Spread a generous amount of remoulade sauce on the bottom half of each baguette or po'boy roll.

- Layer shredded lettuce, sliced tomatoes, and sliced pickles on top of the sauce.

- Arrange the fried oysters on top of the vegetables.

- Drizzle additional remoulade sauce over the oysters if desired.
- Place the top half of the baguette or po'boy roll on top of the assembled sandwich.

5. Serve:

- Serve the Oyster Po'boys immediately, accompanied by lemon wedges for squeezing over the oysters.
- Enjoy your delicious New Orleans-style Oyster Po'boys with a side of coleslaw or potato chips!

Enjoy your delicious New Orleans-style Oyster Po'boys, packed with crispy fried oysters, tangy remoulade sauce, and fresh veggies!

Whether you're hosting a Mardi Gras party, craving a taste of Southern comfort food, or simply looking to expand your culinary horizons, the Oyster Po'boy is sure to be a hit with your family and friends. So why not bring a taste of New Orleans into your own kitchen with this easy-to-make recipe? Your taste buds will thank you.

Shrimp and Grits

Shrimp and grits is a classic dish that perfectly embodies the flavors of New Orleans. It combines the richness of seafood with the heartiness of grits, creating a dish that is both comforting and satisfying.

Ingredients:

For the Grits:

- 1 cup stone-ground grits
- 4 cups water or chicken broth
- Salt and pepper to taste
- 2 tablespoons unsalted butter
- 1/2 cup shredded cheddar cheese (optional)

For the Shrimp:

- 1 pound large shrimp, peeled and deveined
- 1 tablespoon Cajun seasoning
- 2 tablespoons olive oil
- 4 slices bacon, diced
- 1 small onion, finely chopped
- 1 bell pepper, finely chopped
- 2 cloves garlic, minced
- 1 cup chicken broth
- 1 tablespoon Worcestershire sauce
- 1 tablespoon hot sauce (such as Tabasco)
- 2 tablespoons chopped fresh parsley
- Salt and pepper to taste
- Lemon wedges, for serving

Instructions:

1. Prepare the Grits:

- In a medium saucepan, bring the water or chicken broth to a boil.
- Gradually whisk in the grits, stirring constantly to prevent lumps from forming.
- Reduce the heat to low and simmer, stirring occasionally, until the grits are thickened and creamy, about 20-25 minutes.

- Stir in the butter and shredded cheddar cheese (if using) until melted and well combined.
- Season the grits with salt and pepper to taste. Keep warm while you prepare the shrimp.

2. Cook the Shrimp:

- In a medium bowl, toss the peeled and deveined shrimp with Cajun seasoning until evenly coated.
- Heat olive oil in a large skillet over medium-high heat. Add the diced bacon and cook until crispy.
- Remove the bacon from the skillet with a slotted spoon and set aside, leaving the bacon drippings in the skillet.
- Add the seasoned shrimp to the skillet and cook for 2-3 minutes per side, or until pink and opaque. Remove the shrimp from the skillet and set aside.

3. Make the Sauce:

- In the same skillet, add the chopped onion and bell pepper. Cook until softened, about 5-7 minutes.

- Add the minced garlic and cook for an additional 1-2 minutes, until fragrant.

- Pour in the chicken broth, Worcestershire sauce, and hot sauce. Bring the mixture to a simmer and cook for 2-3 minutes to reduce slightly.

- Stir in the cooked bacon and chopped parsley. Season with salt and pepper to taste.

4. Serve:

- Divide the creamy grits among serving bowls.
- Top the grits with the cooked shrimp.
- Spoon the sauce over the shrimp and garnish with additional chopped parsley.
- Serve the New Orleans-style Shrimp and Grits hot, with lemon wedges on the side for squeezing over the shrimp.

Enjoy your delicious New Orleans-style Shrimp and Grits, packed with bold flavors and creamy textures!

Whether you're looking to impress your guests at a Mardi Gras party or simply craving some Southern comfort food, shrimp and grits is sure to hit the spot. So grab your apron and get ready to experience the flavors of New Orleans with this mouthwatering recipe.

Chapter 4: Gumbo Galore

Chicken and Sausage Gumbo

For those outside of New Orleans looking to bring a taste of the Big Easy into their own homes, Chicken and Sausage Gumbo is a classic dish that will transport your taste buds straight to the heart of Louisiana. This hearty and flavorful stew is a staple in New Orleans cuisine, blending the rich flavors of Cajun and Creole cooking for a truly unforgettable dining experience.

Ingredients:

For the Roux:

- 1 cup vegetable oil or bacon fat
- 1 cup all-purpose flour

For the Gumbo:

- 1 whole chicken (about 3-4 pounds), cut into pieces
- 1 pound Andouille sausage, sliced into rounds

- 1 large onion, diced
- 1 green bell pepper, diced
- 2 celery stalks, diced
- 4 cloves garlic, minced
- 1 cup sliced okra (fresh or frozen) (optional)
- 1 can (14.5 ounces) diced tomatoes
- 8 cups chicken broth (preferably homemade or low-sodium)
- 2 bay leaves
- 2 teaspoons Cajun seasoning (adjust to taste)
- Salt and pepper to taste
- 2 tablespoons file powder (optional, for thickening)
- Cooked white rice, for serving
- Chopped green onions, for garnish

Instructions:

1. Make the Roux:

- In a large, heavy-bottomed pot or Dutch oven, heat the vegetable oil or bacon fat over medium heat.

- Gradually add the flour to the hot oil, stirring constantly to combine.

- Continue to cook the flour and oil mixture, stirring frequently, until it turns a rich caramel color. This process can take anywhere from 30 minutes to an hour. Be careful not to burn it.

2. Brown the Chicken and Sausage:

- In the same pot used for the roux, add the Andouille sausage slices. Cook them over medium heat until they are browned and release their flavorful oils, about 5-7 minutes. Remove the sausage from the pot and set aside.
- Add the chicken pieces to the pot and brown them on all sides, working in batches if necessary to avoid overcrowding the pot. Remove the chicken from the pot and set aside.

3. Cook the Aromatics:

- In the same pot, add the diced onion, bell pepper, and celery. Cook, stirring occasionally, until the vegetables are softened and translucent, about 5-7 minutes.

- Add the minced garlic to the pot and cook for an additional 1-2 minutes, until fragrant.

4. Combine Ingredients:

- Return the browned sausage and chicken to the pot with the cooked vegetables.
- Add the sliced okra (if using), diced tomatoes, chicken broth, bay leaves, and Cajun seasoning to the pot, stirring to combine.

5. Simmer the Gumbo:

Bring the gumbo to a boil, then reduce the heat to low and let it simmer, uncovered, for about 1-1.5 hours, stirring occasionally. This allows the flavors to meld together and the chicken to become tender.

6. Thicken the Gumbo:

If desired, sprinkle the file powder over the gumbo and stir well to incorporate. Let the gumbo simmer for an additional 10-15 minutes to thicken.

7. Serve:

- Serve the Chicken and Sausage Gumbo hot over cooked white rice.
- Garnish each serving with chopped green onions.

Enjoy your delicious New Orleans-style Chicken and Sausage Gumbo!

Whether you're celebrating Mardi Gras, hosting a Southern comfort food feast, or simply craving a taste of the Bayou, Chicken and Sausage Gumbo is the perfect dish to satisfy your cravings for New Orleans cuisine. So grab your apron, fire up the stove, and get ready to jambalaya jamboree with this mouthwatering recipe!

Seafood Gumbo

For folks outside New Orleans, the thought of making a traditional Seafood Gumbo may seem like a daunting task. However, with the right recipe and a little bit of patience, you can easily recreate this classic Creole dish in your own kitchen.

Ingredients:

For the Roux:

- 1 cup vegetable oil or bacon fat
- 1 cup all-purpose flour

For the Gumbo:

- 1 pound shrimp, peeled and deveined, shells reserved
- 1 pound crab legs or crabmeat
- 1 pound okra, sliced (fresh or frozen)
- 1 cup diced onion
- 1 cup diced bell pepper
- 1 cup diced celery
- 4 cloves garlic, minced
- 1 (14.5 oz) can diced tomatoes, undrained

- 8 cups seafood stock or chicken broth
- 2 bay leaves
- 1 teaspoon dried thyme
- 1 teaspoon dried oregano
- 1 teaspoon smoked paprika
- 1/2 teaspoon cayenne pepper (adjust to taste)

- Salt and pepper to taste
- 1 tablespoon Worcestershire sauce
- 1 tablespoon hot sauce (such as Tabasco)
- 1/4 cup chopped fresh parsley
- 1/4 cup chopped green onions
- Cooked white rice, for serving

Instructions:

1. Prepare the Roux:

- In a heavy-bottomed Dutch oven or large pot, heat the vegetable oil or bacon fat over medium heat.

- Gradually whisk in the all-purpose flour, stirring constantly to prevent lumps from forming.

- Continue cooking the roux, stirring frequently, until it reaches a dark brown color, similar to chocolate, about 30-40 minutes. Be careful not to burn the roux, as it can easily become bitter.

2. Cook the Aromatics:

- Once the roux has reached the desired color, add the diced onion, bell pepper, celery, and minced garlic to the pot.
- Cook the vegetables, stirring occasionally, until they are softened, about 5-7 minutes.

3. Add the Tomatoes and Stock:

- Stir in the diced tomatoes (with their juices) and seafood stock or chicken broth.
- Add the bay leaves, dried thyme, dried oregano, smoked paprika, cayenne pepper, salt, and pepper.
- Bring the mixture to a simmer, then reduce the heat to low and let it cook for about 30 minutes to allow the flavors to meld together.

4. Add the Seafood and Okra:

- Once the gumbo base has simmered, add the reserved shrimp shells to the pot to infuse additional flavor.
- Stir in the sliced okra and continue simmering for another 15-20 minutes, or until the okra is tender.

5. Finish the Gumbo:

- Remove and discard the bay leaves and shrimp shells from the gumbo.
- Stir in the Worcestershire sauce, hot sauce, chopped parsley, and chopped green onions.
- Add the peeled shrimp and crab legs or crabmeat to the pot.
- Simmer the gumbo for an additional 5-7 minutes, or until the shrimp are pink and cooked through.
- Taste and adjust the seasoning with additional salt, pepper, or hot sauce if desired.

6. Serve:

- Ladle the New Orleans-style Seafood Gumbo into serving bowls.
- Serve the gumbo hot, over cooked white rice.

Enjoy your delicious New Orleans-style Seafood Gumbo, packed with rich flavors and tender seafood!

This dish is perfect for a Mardi Gras celebration, a cozy night in, or any occasion that calls for some comfort food. So grab your apron and get ready to impress your friends and family with this delicious Creole creation.

Okra Gumbo

Are you looking to bring a taste of New Orleans into your kitchen? Look no further than the classic Southern comfort food dish known as Okra Gumbo. This flavorful and hearty stew is a staple in Creole and Cajun cuisine, and is sure to be a hit with your family and friends.

Ingredients:

For the Roux:

- 1/2 cup vegetable oil or bacon fat
- 1/2 cup all-purpose flour

For the Gumbo:

- 1 pound fresh okra, sliced
- 1 pound chicken thighs or drumsticks, bone-in and skin-on
- 1 pound smoked sausage (such as Andouille), sliced
- 1 cup diced onion
- 1 cup diced bell pepper
- 1 cup diced celery
- 4 cloves garlic, minced
- 1 (14.5 oz) can diced tomatoes, undrained
- 8 cups chicken broth
- 2 bay leaves
- 1 teaspoon dried thyme
- 1 teaspoon dried oregano
- 1 teaspoon smoked paprika
- 1/2 teaspoon cayenne pepper (adjust to taste)
- Salt and pepper to taste
- 1 tablespoon Worcestershire sauce
- 1 tablespoon hot sauce (such as Tabasco)
- 1/4 cup chopped fresh parsley
- 1/4 cup chopped green onions
- Cooked white rice, for serving

Instructions:

1. Prepare the Roux:

- In a heavy-bottomed Dutch oven or large pot, heat the vegetable oil or bacon fat over medium heat.

- Gradually whisk in the all-purpose flour, stirring constantly to prevent lumps from forming.

- Continue cooking the roux, stirring frequently, until it reaches a dark brown color, similar to chocolate, about 30-40 minutes. Be careful not to burn the roux, as it can easily become bitter.

2. Cook the Chicken and Sausage:

- While the roux is cooking, season the chicken thighs or drumsticks with salt and pepper.

- In a separate skillet, heat a little oil over medium-high heat.

- Add the seasoned chicken pieces and brown them on all sides, about 5-7 minutes per side.

- Remove the chicken from the skillet and set aside.
- In the same skillet, add the sliced smoked sausage and cook until browned, about 5 minutes. Remove the sausage from the skillet and set aside.

3. Cook the Aromatics:

- Once the roux has reached the desired color, add the diced onion, bell pepper, celery, and minced garlic to the pot.
- Cook the vegetables, stirring occasionally, until they are softened, about 5-7 minutes.

4. Add the Tomatoes and Broth:

- Stir in the diced tomatoes (with their juices) and chicken broth.
- Add the bay leaves, dried thyme, dried oregano, smoked paprika, cayenne pepper, salt, and pepper.
- Bring the mixture to a simmer, then reduce the heat to low and let it cook for about 30 minutes to allow the flavors to meld together.

5. Add the Okra:

- Once the gumbo base has simmered, add the sliced okra to the pot.
- Continue simmering for another 15-20 minutes, or until the okra is tender.

6. Finish the Gumbo:

- Remove and discard the bay leaves from the gumbo.
- Stir in the Worcestershire sauce, hot sauce, chopped parsley, and chopped green onions.
- Return the cooked chicken and smoked sausage to the pot.
- Simmer the gumbo for an additional 5-7 minutes to heat through.

7. Serve:

- Ladle the New Orleans-style Okra Gumbo into serving bowls.
- Serve the gumbo hot, over cooked white rice.

Enjoy your delicious New Orleans-style Okra Gumbo, packed with rich flavors and tender chicken and sausage!

This dish is perfect for a cozy night in or for a festive Mardi Gras celebration. So grab your apron and get ready to experience the flavors of New Orleans with this delicious and easy-to-make Okra Gumbo recipe.

File Gumbo

For folks outside of New Orleans, the mention of "File Gumbo" may bring to mind a thick, flavorful stew filled with seafood, smoked sausage, and okra. And they wouldn't be wrong! File Gumbo is a classic New Orleans dish that perfectly encapsulates the city's rich culinary heritage.

Ingredients:

For the Roux:

- 1/2 cup vegetable oil or bacon fat
- 1/2 cup all-purpose flour

For the Gumbo:

- 1 pound chicken thighs or drumsticks, bone-in and skin-on
- 1 pound smoked sausage (such as Andouille), sliced
- 1 cup diced onion
- 1 cup diced bell pepper
- 1 cup diced celery

- 4 cloves garlic, minced
- 1 (14.5 oz) can diced tomatoes, undrained
- 8 cups chicken broth
- 2 bay leaves
- 1 teaspoon dried thyme
- 1 teaspoon dried oregano
- 1 teaspoon smoked paprika
- 1/2 teaspoon cayenne pepper (adjust to taste)

- Salt and pepper to taste
- 1 tablespoon Worcestershire sauce
- 1 tablespoon hot sauce (such as Tabasco)
- 1/4 cup chopped fresh parsley
- 1/4 cup chopped green onions
- 2 tablespoons file powder
- Cooked white rice, for serving

Instructions:

1. Prepare the Roux:

- In a heavy-bottomed Dutch oven or large pot, heat the vegetable oil or bacon fat over medium heat.
- Gradually whisk in the all-purpose flour, stirring constantly to prevent lumps from forming.
- Continue cooking the roux, stirring frequently, until it reaches a dark brown color, similar to chocolate, about 30-40 minutes. Be careful not to burn the roux, as it can easily become bitter.

2. Cook the Chicken and Sausage:

- While the roux is cooking, season the chicken thighs or drumsticks with salt and pepper.
- In a separate skillet, heat a little oil over medium-high heat.
- Add the seasoned chicken pieces and brown them on all sides, about 5-7 minutes per side.
- Remove the chicken from the skillet and set aside.
- In the same skillet, add the sliced smoked sausage and cook until browned, about 5 minutes. Remove the sausage from the skillet and set aside.

3. Cook the Aromatics:

- Once the roux has reached the desired color, add the diced onion, bell pepper, celery, and minced garlic to the pot.

- Cook the vegetables, stirring occasionally, until they are softened, about 5-7 minutes.

4. Add the Tomatoes and Broth:

- Stir in the diced tomatoes (with their juices) and chicken broth.
- Add the bay leaves, dried thyme, dried oregano, smoked paprika, cayenne pepper, salt, and pepper.
- Bring the mixture to a simmer, then reduce the heat to low and let it cook for about 30 minutes to allow the flavors to meld together.

5. Finish the Gumbo:

- Remove and discard the bay leaves from
  the gumbo.
- Return the cooked chicken and smoked
  sausage to the pot.
- Stir in the Worcestershire sauce, hot
  sauce, chopped parsley, and chopped
  green onions.
- Simmer the gumbo for an additional 5-7
  minutes to heat through.

6. Add the File Powder:

- Just before serving, sprinkle the file
  powder over the gumbo and stir until
  well combined.
- File powder is a thickening agent and
  should not be boiled or cooked for too
  long, as it can become stringy.

7. Serve:

- Ladle the New Orleans-style File Gumbo
  into serving bowls.
- Serve the gumbo hot, over cooked white
  rice.

Enjoy your delicious New Orleans-style File
Gumbo, packed with rich flavors and tender
chicken and sausage!

So grab your apron and get ready to dive into the world of New Orleans cuisine with our File Gumbo recipe. Your taste buds will thank you!

Chapter 5: Jambalaya Jamboree

Chicken and Andouille Sausage Jambalaya

For folks outside of New Orleans looking to bring a taste of the Big Easy into their homes, there's no better dish than Chicken and Andouille Sausage Jambalaya. This classic Creole dish is a staple in New Orleans cuisine and is sure to impress your family and friends.

Ingredients:

- 1 pound boneless, skinless chicken thighs, cut into bite-sized pieces
- 1 pound Andouille sausage, sliced into rounds
- 1 large onion, diced
- 1 bell pepper, diced
- 2 stalks celery, diced
- 3 cloves garlic, minced
- 1 can (14.5 oz) diced tomatoes

- 3 cups chicken broth
- 1 1/2 cups long-grain white rice
- 2 bay leaves
- 1 teaspoon dried thyme
- 1 teaspoon paprika
- 1/2 teaspoon cayenne pepper (adjust to taste)
- Salt and black pepper to taste
- Chopped fresh parsley, for garnish
- Sliced green onions, for garnish

Instructions:

1. Brown the Chicken and Sausage:

- Heat a large Dutch oven or heavy-bottomed pot over medium-high heat.
- Add the Andouille sausage slices and cook until they are browned on both sides. Remove from the pot and set aside.
- In the same pot, add the chicken pieces and cook until they are browned on all sides. Remove from the pot and set aside.

2. Sauté the Vegetables:

- In the same pot, add the diced onion, bell pepper, and celery. Sauté until the vegetables are softened, about 5-7 minutes.

- Add the minced garlic and cook for an additional 1-2 minutes until fragrant.

3. Add the Tomatoes and Spices:

- Stir in the diced tomatoes (with their juices) and cook for 2-3 minutes.
- Add the bay leaves, dried thyme, paprika, cayenne pepper, salt, and black pepper. Stir to combine.

4. Simmer with Broth and Rice:

- Return the browned chicken and Andouille sausage to the pot.
- Pour in the chicken broth and bring the mixture to a boil.
- Stir in the long-grain white rice, reduce the heat to low, cover, and simmer for about 20-25 minutes, or until the rice is cooked through and the liquid is absorbed.

5. Let it Rest:

Once the rice is cooked, remove the pot from the heat and let it rest, covered, for 5-10 minutes.

6. Serve:

- Fluff the jambalaya with a fork and remove the bay leaves.
- Garnish with chopped fresh parsley and sliced green onions before serving.

Enjoy your flavorful New Orleans-style Chicken and Andouille Sausage Jambalaya, packed with Cajun spices and hearty ingredients!

Whether you're hosting a Mardi Gras party or simply craving some Southern comfort food, Chicken and Andouille Sausage Jambalaya is a crowd-pleasing dish that will have everyone coming back for seconds. So grab a pot, gather your ingredients, and get ready to experience the flavors of New Orleans in your own home. Bon appétit!

Seafood Jambalaya

Seafood Jambalaya is a quintessential New Orleans dish that combines the bold flavors of Cajun and Creole cuisine with the fresh seafood that the Gulf Coast is famous for. This hearty and satisfying one-pot meal is perfect for any occasion, from a weeknight dinner to a festive Mardi Gras celebration.

Ingredients:

- 1 pound large shrimp, peeled and deveined
- 1 pound scallops
- 1 pound mussels, cleaned and debearded
- 1 pound firm white fish fillets (such as cod or snapper), cut into bite-sized pieces
- 1 pound Andouille sausage, sliced
- 1 large onion, diced
- 1 bell pepper, diced
- 2 stalks celery, diced
- 4 cloves garlic, minced
- 1 (14.5 oz) can diced tomatoes, undrained
- 2 cups long-grain white rice
- 4 cups chicken broth or seafood stock
- 2 bay leaves

- 1 teaspoon dried thyme
- 1 teaspoon dried oregano
- 1 teaspoon smoked paprika
- 1/2 teaspoon cayenne pepper (adjust to taste)
- Salt and pepper to taste
- 2 tablespoons olive oil
- Chopped fresh parsley, for garnish
- Lemon wedges, for serving

Instructions:

1. Prepare the Seafood:

- Season the shrimp, scallops, mussels, and fish fillets with salt and pepper.
- Set aside while you prepare the rest of the ingredients.

2. Cook the Sausage:

- Heat olive oil in a large Dutch oven or heavy-bottomed pot over medium heat.
- Add the sliced Andouille sausage and cook until browned, about 5 minutes.
- Remove the sausage from the pot and set aside.

3. Cook the Aromatics:

- In the same pot, add the diced onion, bell pepper, and celery. Cook until softened, about 5-7 minutes.
- Add the minced garlic and cook for an additional 1-2 minutes until fragrant.

4. Add the Rice and Spices:

- Stir in the long-grain white rice, diced tomatoes (with their juices), chicken broth or seafood stock, bay leaves, dried thyme, dried oregano, smoked paprika, and cayenne pepper.
- Season with salt and pepper to taste.
- Bring the mixture to a boil, then reduce the heat to low, cover, and simmer for 15 minutes.

5. Add the Seafood and Sausage:

- After 15 minutes of cooking the rice, add the browned Andouille sausage back to the pot.
- Gently stir in the seasoned shrimp, scallops, mussels, and fish fillets.

- Cover the pot and continue simmering for an additional 10-12 minutes, or until the seafood is cooked through and the mussels have opened.
- Discard any mussels that do not open.

6. Serve:

- Remove the pot from the heat and discard the bay leaves.
- Garnish the New Orleans-style Seafood Jambalaya with chopped fresh parsley.
- Serve the jambalaya hot, with lemon wedges on the side for squeezing over the seafood.

Enjoy your delicious New Orleans-style Seafood Jambalaya, packed with flavorful seafood and aromatic spices!

Whether you're a seasoned pro at making New Orleans recipes or a newbie looking to explore the vibrant flavors of Southern comfort food, Seafood Jambalaya is sure to be a hit with your friends and family. So grab a pot, gather your ingredients, and get ready to enjoy a taste of the Big Easy right in your own home.

Vegetarian Jambalaya

For folks outside of New Orleans looking to experience the authentic flavors of the Big Easy, there's no better dish to try than Vegetarian Jambalaya. This classic Creole dish is a staple in New Orleans cuisine, known for its bold spices and rich flavors.

While traditional jambalaya typically includes a variety of meats, this vegetarian version is just as delicious and satisfying. By using hearty vegetables like bell peppers, onions, and celery, along with protein-packed beans and flavorful spices, you can create a dish that is sure to impress even the biggest carnivores.

Ingredients:

- 2 tablespoons olive oil
- 1 large onion, diced
- 1 bell pepper, diced
- 2 stalks celery, diced
- 3 cloves garlic, minced
- 1 (14.5 oz) can diced tomatoes, undrained

- 1 cup long-grain white rice
- 2 cups vegetable broth or water
- 1 (15 oz) can kidney beans, drained and rinsed
- 1 cup corn kernels (fresh, frozen, or canned)
- 1 cup diced zucchini
- 1 cup diced eggplant
- 1 teaspoon smoked paprika
- 1/2 teaspoon dried thyme
- 1/2 teaspoon dried oregano
- 1/4 teaspoon cayenne pepper (adjust to taste)
- Salt and pepper to taste
- Chopped fresh parsley, for garnish
- Lemon wedges, for serving

Instructions:

1. Sauté the Vegetables:

- Heat olive oil in a large skillet or Dutch oven over medium heat.
- Add the diced onion, bell pepper, and celery to the skillet. Cook until softened, about 5-7 minutes.
- Add the minced garlic and cook for an additional 1-2 minutes until fragrant.

2. Add the Rice and Tomatoes:

- Stir in the long-grain white rice and diced tomatoes (with their juices) into the skillet.
- Pour in the vegetable broth or water and bring the mixture to a boil.
- Reduce the heat to low, cover, and simmer for 15 minutes.

3. Add the Beans and Vegetables:

- After 15 minutes of cooking the rice, add the drained and rinsed kidney beans, corn kernels, diced zucchini, and diced eggplant to the skillet.
- Season with smoked paprika, dried thyme, dried oregano, cayenne pepper, salt, and pepper.
- Stir to combine, cover, and continue simmering for an additional 10-15 minutes, or until the rice is tender and the vegetables are cooked through.

4. Serve:

- Remove the skillet from the heat and give the Vegetarian Jambalaya a final stir.
- Garnish with chopped fresh parsley.
- Serve the jambalaya hot, with lemon wedges on the side for squeezing over the dish.

Enjoy your flavorful New Orleans-style Vegetarian Jambalaya, packed with a variety of vegetables and aromatic spices!

Whether you're a seasoned pro at making New Orleans recipes or are just starting out on your culinary journey, this Vegetarian Jambalaya is sure to become a new favorite in your repertoire. So grab a pot, turn up the jazz music, and get cooking - you'll feel like you're celebrating Mardi Gras year-round with each delicious bite.

Creole Jambalaya

Creole Jambalaya is a quintessential New Orleans dish that perfectly captures the essence of this vibrant city's cuisine. For folks outside New Orleans, this flavorful and hearty dish is a must-try, as it combines the best of Cajun and Creole flavors in one delicious pot.

Ingredients:

- 2 tablespoons vegetable oil
- 1 pound Andouille sausage, sliced
- 1 pound boneless, skinless chicken thighs or breasts, cut into bite-sized pieces
- 1 large onion, diced
- 1 bell pepper, diced
- 2 stalks celery, diced
- 3 cloves garlic, minced
- 1 (14.5 oz) can diced tomatoes, undrained
- 1 cup long-grain white rice
- 2 cups chicken broth or vegetable broth
- 1 teaspoon smoked paprika
- 1 teaspoon dried thyme
- 1 teaspoon dried oregano
- 1/2 teaspoon cayenne pepper (adjust to taste)
- Salt and pepper to taste

- 1 pound shrimp, peeled and deveined
- Chopped fresh parsley, for garnish
- Lemon wedges, for serving

Instructions:

1. Sauté the Sausage and Chicken:

- Heat vegetable oil in a large skillet or Dutch oven over medium heat.
- Add the sliced Andouille sausage to the skillet and cook until browned, about 5 minutes.
- Remove the sausage from the skillet and set aside.
- In the same skillet, add the bite-sized chicken pieces and cook until browned on all sides, about 5-7 minutes.
- Remove the chicken from the skillet and set aside.

2. Cook the Aromatics:

- In the same skillet, add the diced onion, bell pepper, and celery. Cook until softened, about 5-7 minutes.
- Add the minced garlic and cook for an additional 1-2 minutes until fragrant.

3. Add the Rice and Tomatoes:

- Stir in the long-grain white rice and diced tomatoes (with their juices) into the skillet.
- Pour in the chicken broth or vegetable broth and bring the mixture to a boil.
- Reduce the heat to low, cover, and simmer for 15 minutes.

4. Add the Spices and Protein:

- After 15 minutes of cooking the rice, add the cooked Andouille sausage back to the skillet.
- Season with smoked paprika, dried thyme, dried oregano, cayenne pepper, salt, and pepper.
- Stir to combine, cover, and continue simmering for another 10-15 minutes, or until the rice is tender and the flavors have melded together.
- Add the peeled and deveined shrimp to the skillet during the last 5 minutes of cooking, stirring occasionally, until the shrimp are pink and cooked through.

5. Serve:

- Remove the skillet from the heat and give the Creole Jambalaya a final stir.
- Garnish with chopped fresh parsley.
- Serve the jambalaya hot, with lemon wedges on the side for squeezing over the dish.

Enjoy your delicious New Orleans-style Creole Jambalaya, packed with savory sausage, tender chicken, and succulent shrimp!

Whether you're celebrating Mardi Gras, hosting a Southern-inspired dinner party, or simply craving a taste of New Orleans, Creole Jambalaya is sure to please. So grab your largest pot, gather your ingredients, and get ready to experience the magic of this iconic dish from the Big Easy.

Chapter 6: Mardi Gras Madness

King Cake

King Cake is a beloved tradition in New Orleans, especially during the festive season of Mardi Gras. This sweet and colorful cake is a symbol of the carnival season and is enjoyed by locals and visitors alike. For folks outside New Orleans who may not be familiar with this delicious treat, let me introduce you to the joy of King Cake.

King Cake is a sweet bread-like cake that is typically oval-shaped and decorated with purple, green, and gold colored icing or sugar. These colors represent justice, faith, and power, which are the traditional colors of Mardi Gras. The cake also contains a hidden plastic baby figurine, and whoever finds the baby in their slice is said to have good luck for the coming year.

Ingredients:

For the Dough:

- 1 cup warm milk (110°F/45°C)
- 2 (1/4 oz) packages active dry yeast
- 1/2 cup granulated sugar
- 1/2 cup unsalted butter, melted
- 5 egg yolks
- 1 teaspoon vanilla extract
- 1 teaspoon grated lemon zest
- 1/2 teaspoon ground nutmeg
- 1/2 teaspoon salt
- 4 to 4 1/2 cups all-purpose flour

For the Filling:

- 1/2 cup brown sugar, packed
- 1/2 cup granulated sugar
- 1 tablespoon ground cinnamon
- 1/2 cup unsalted butter, softened
- 1 cup chopped pecans (optional)

For the Glaze:

- 2 cups powdered sugar
- 2-3 tablespoons milk
- 1 teaspoon vanilla extract
- Purple, green, and yellow food coloring

For the Decoration:

- Colored sugar (purple, green, and yellow)
- Small plastic baby figurine (optional)

Instructions:

1. Prepare the Dough:

- In a large mixing bowl, dissolve the yeast in warm milk and let it sit for 5-10 minutes until frothy.
- Add the granulated sugar, melted butter, egg yolks, vanilla extract, lemon zest, nutmeg, and salt to the yeast mixture. Mix until well combined.
- Gradually add 4 cups of all-purpose flour, one cup at a time, stirring until a soft dough forms.
- If the dough is too sticky, gradually add more flour until it pulls away from the sides of the bowl.
- Turn the dough out onto a floured surface and knead for 5-7 minutes until smooth and elastic.
- Place the dough in a greased bowl, cover with a clean kitchen towel, and let it rise in a warm place for about 1-2 hours or until doubled in size.

2. Make the Filling:

- In a small bowl, combine the brown sugar, granulated sugar, and ground cinnamon.
- Cut the softened butter into small pieces and mix it into the sugar mixture until crumbly. Stir in the chopped pecans if using.

3. Assemble the King Cake:

- Punch down the risen dough and turn it out onto a floured surface.
- Roll the dough into a large rectangle, about 10x20 inches in size.
- Spread the filling evenly over the dough, leaving a small border around the edges.
- Starting from one long edge, roll the dough tightly into a log.
- Pinch the seams to seal and shape the log into a ring or oval shape.
- Place the shaped dough on a parchment-lined baking sheet and cover with a clean kitchen towel. Let it rise for another 30-45 minutes.

4. Bake the King Cake:

- Preheat the oven to 350°F (175°C).
- Bake the risen King Cake in the preheated oven for 25-30 minutes, or until golden brown and cooked through.
- Remove the King Cake from the oven and let it cool completely on a wire rack.

5. Make the Glaze:

- In a medium bowl, whisk together the powdered sugar, milk, and vanilla extract until smooth.
- Divide the glaze into three portions and tint each portion with purple, green, and yellow food coloring.

6. Decorate the King Cake:

- Once the King Cake has cooled, drizzle the colored glazes over the top of the cake in a random pattern.
- Sprinkle colored sugar over the glaze while it's still wet, alternating between purple, green, and yellow.
- If desired, insert a small plastic baby figurine into the bottom of the cake.

7. Serve:

Slice the King Cake and serve at room temperature.

Enjoy your festive New Orleans-style King Cake, traditionally served during Mardi Gras celebrations!

Whether you're celebrating Mardi Gras or just looking to add a bit of New Orleans flavor to your day, King Cake is a must-try.

Mardi Gras Beignets

Folks outside of New Orleans, get ready to indulge in the deliciousness of Mardi Gras Beignets! These delectable treats are a staple during the festive season in the Big Easy, and now you can bring a taste of Mardi Gras into your own home with this easy-to-follow recipe.

Beignets are deep-fried pastries that are light, fluffy, and covered in a generous dusting of powdered sugar. They are perfect for breakfast, brunch, or as a sweet treat any time of day. The best part is, you don't have to wait for Mardi Gras to enjoy these mouthwatering pastries – you can make them at home whenever the craving strikes!

Mardi Gras Beignets

Ingredients:

- 1 cup lukewarm water (about 110°F/45°C)
- 1/4 cup granulated sugar
- 2 1/4 teaspoons (1 packet) active dry yeast
- 1 teaspoon salt
- 2 large eggs

- 1/2 cup evaporated milk
- 4 cups all-purpose flour, plus extra for dusting

- Vegetable oil, for frying
- Powdered sugar, for dusting

Instructions:

1. Activate the Yeast:

In a large mixing bowl, combine the lukewarm water and granulated sugar. Sprinkle the active dry yeast over the water and let it sit for about 5-10 minutes until frothy.

2. Mix the Dough:

- Once the yeast is activated, add the salt, eggs, and evaporated milk to the bowl. Stir until well combined.
- Gradually add the all-purpose flour, one cup at a time, stirring until a soft dough forms.
- Turn the dough out onto a floured surface and knead for 5-7 minutes until smooth and elastic.

3. Let the Dough Rise:

- Place the kneaded dough in a greased bowl and cover it with a clean kitchen towel or plastic wrap.
- Let the dough rise in a warm place for about 1-2 hours, or until doubled in size.

4. Roll and Cut the Beignets:

- Once the dough has doubled in size, punch it down and turn it out onto a floured surface.
- Roll the dough out into a large rectangle, about 1/4 inch thick.
- Use a sharp knife or pizza cutter to cut the dough into squares, about 2-3 inches in size.

5. Fry the Beignets:

- In a large, deep pot or Dutch oven, heat vegetable oil to 350°F (175°C).
- Carefully drop a few pieces of dough into the hot oil, being careful not to overcrowd the pot.

- Fry the beignets for 2-3 minutes on each side, or until they are golden brown and puffed up.
- Use a slotted spoon or spider strainer to remove the beignets from the oil and transfer them to a paper towel-lined plate to drain excess oil.

6. Serve:

- Once all the beignets are fried, dust them generously with powdered sugar while they are still warm.
- Serve the Mardi Gras Beignets immediately, while they are fresh and warm.

Enjoy your delicious New Orleans-style Mardi Gras Beignets, perfect for celebrating Fat Tuesday or any festive occasion!

These Mardi Gras Beignets are perfect for serving at a Mardi Gras celebration, brunch with friends, or simply as a special treat for yourself. Pair them with a hot cup of coffee or a glass of cold milk for the ultimate indulgence.

So go ahead, bring a taste of New Orleans into your kitchen with these irresistible Mardi Gras Beignets. Your taste buds will thank you!

Cajun Dirty Rice

For folks outside New Orleans looking to bring a taste of the Big Easy into their own kitchen, Cajun Dirty Rice is a must-try dish that captures the essence of Creole cuisine. This traditional New Orleans recipe is a flavorful and hearty dish that is perfect for any occasion.

Ingredients:

- 1 cup long-grain white rice
- 2 cups chicken broth or vegetable broth
- 1 pound ground beef or pork
- 1/2 pound Andouille sausage, diced
- 1 onion, finely chopped
- 1 bell pepper, finely chopped
- 2 stalks celery, finely chopped
- 3 cloves garlic, minced

- 2 green onions, thinly sliced
- 2 tablespoons vegetable oil
- 1 tablespoon Cajun seasoning
- 1/2 teaspoon paprika
- 1/2 teaspoon dried thyme
- Salt and pepper to taste
- Hot sauce, for serving
- Chopped fresh parsley, for garnish

Instructions:

1. Cook the Rice:

- Rinse the long-grain white rice under cold water until the water runs clear.
- In a saucepan, bring the chicken broth or vegetable broth to a boil.
- Add the rinsed rice to the boiling broth, cover, and reduce the heat to low.
- Simmer the rice for 15-20 minutes, or until it is cooked through and the liquid is absorbed. Remove from heat and set aside.

2. Brown the Meat:

- In a large skillet or Dutch oven, heat the vegetable oil over medium-high heat.

- Add the ground beef or pork to the skillet and cook, breaking it up with a spoon, until browned and cooked through.
- Add the diced Andouille sausage to the skillet and cook for an additional 3-4 minutes, until it is lightly browned.

3. Sauté the Vegetables:

- Add the chopped onion, bell pepper, and celery to the skillet with the meat.
- Cook, stirring occasionally, until the vegetables are softened, about 5-7 minutes.
- Add the minced garlic to the skillet and cook for an additional 1-2 minutes, until fragrant.

4. Season the Rice:

- Stir the cooked rice into the skillet with the meat and vegetables.
- Season the mixture with Cajun seasoning, paprika, dried thyme, salt, and pepper.
- Mix well to combine all the ingredients evenly.

5. Finish and Serve:

- Cook the dirty rice mixture for an additional 5-7 minutes, stirring occasionally, to allow the flavors to meld together.

- Taste and adjust the seasoning with salt, pepper, or additional Cajun seasoning if desired.

- Garnish the Cajun Dirty Rice with thinly sliced green onions and chopped fresh parsley.
- Serve hot, with hot sauce on the side for those who like it spicy.

Enjoy your flavorful New Orleans-style Cajun Dirty Rice, packed with savory meat, aromatic vegetables, and Cajun spices!

Cajun Dirty Rice is a versatile dish that can be served as a main course or as a side dish to accompany other New Orleans favorites like gumbo or jambalaya. It is a popular dish during Mardi Gras celebrations and is sure to be a hit at any Southern-themed party.

So, whether you're craving a taste of the Bayou or just looking to explore the flavors of New Orleans cuisine, Cajun Dirty Rice is a delicious and easy-to-make dish that is sure to please your taste buds. Give this recipe a try and transport yourself to the streets of New Orleans with every flavorful bite.

Corn Maque Choux

Corn Maque Choux is a classic dish in New Orleans cuisine that combines the flavors of sweet corn, bell peppers, onions, and spices to create a delicious and hearty side dish. This dish is perfect for any occasion, whether you're hosting a Mardi Gras party or simply looking to add a touch of New Orleans flavor to your dinner table.

Corn Maque Choux

Ingredients:

- 4 ears of fresh corn, husked and kernels cut off the cob
- 1 tablespoon vegetable oil
- 1/2 pound Andouille sausage, diced
- 1 onion, diced
- 1 bell pepper, diced
- 2 stalks celery, diced
- 2 cloves garlic, minced
- 1 tomato, diced
- 1/2 cup chicken broth or vegetable broth

- 1/2 cup heavy cream
- 1 teaspoon Cajun seasoning
- Salt and pepper to taste
- Chopped fresh parsley, for garnish

Instructions:

1. Prepare the Corn:

Husk the fresh corn and remove the kernels from the cob using a sharp knife. Set aside.

2. Sauté the Sausage:

- In a large skillet or Dutch oven, heat the vegetable oil over medium-high heat.
- Add the diced Andouille sausage to the skillet and cook until browned, about 5 minutes.

3. Sauté the Vegetables:

- Add the diced onion, bell pepper, and celery to the skillet with the sausage.

- Cook, stirring occasionally, until the vegetables are softened, about 5-7 minutes.

- Add the minced garlic to the skillet and cook for an additional 1-2 minutes, until fragrant.

4. Cook the Corn:

- Stir in the fresh corn kernels and diced tomato into the skillet with the sausage and vegetables.
- Cook, stirring occasionally, for 5-7 minutes, until the corn is tender.

5. Add the Liquid and Seasoning:

- Pour the chicken broth or vegetable broth into the skillet and stir to combine.
- Stir in the heavy cream and Cajun seasoning.
- Season with salt and pepper to taste.

6. Simmer and Serve:

- Reduce the heat to low and simmer the Corn Maque Choux for 10-15 minutes, stirring occasionally, until the flavors meld together and the mixture thickens slightly.

- Taste and adjust the seasoning with salt, pepper, or additional Cajun seasoning if desired.
- Garnish the Corn Maque Choux with chopped fresh parsley before serving.

Enjoy your delicious New Orleans-style Corn Maque Choux, packed with sweet corn, savory Andouille sausage, and aromatic vegetables!

Corn Maque Choux is a great way to experience the flavors of New Orleans without having to leave your own kitchen. Whether you're a fan of Cajun or Creole cuisine, this dish is sure to satisfy your cravings for authentic New Orleans flavors. So why not give it a try and bring a taste of the Big Easy to your next meal?

Chapter 7: Southern Comfort Food Favorites

Boudin Balls

If you've never had the pleasure of trying a Boudin Ball, you're in for a real treat! This classic New Orleans dish is a must-try for anyone looking to experience the true flavors of the Big Easy.

Ingredients:

- 1 pound boudin sausage, removed from casings
- 1 cup all-purpose flour
- 2 large eggs, beaten
- 1 cup fine breadcrumbs
- Vegetable oil, for frying
- Creole seasoning (optional), for seasoning
- Dipping sauce of your choice (such as remoulade or hot sauce)

Instructions:

1. Prepare the Boudin:

If the boudin sausage is in casings, remove the sausage from the casings and place it in a mixing bowl.

2. Shape the Boudin Balls:

Take about 2 tablespoons of the boudin mixture and roll it into a ball using your hands. Repeat with the remaining boudin mixture until you have formed all the balls.

3. Prepare the Dredging Stations:

Set up three shallow bowls or plates: one with the all-purpose flour, one with the beaten eggs, and one with the fine breadcrumbs.

4. Dredge the Boudin Balls:

- Roll each boudin ball in the all-purpose flour, shaking off any excess.
- Dip the floured boudin ball into the beaten eggs, ensuring it is coated on all sides.
- Roll the egg-coated boudin ball in the fine breadcrumbs until it is evenly coated. Repeat with the remaining boudin balls.

5. Fry the Boudin Balls:

- In a deep skillet or Dutch oven, heat vegetable oil to 350°F (175°C) over medium-high heat.
- Carefully place a few boudin balls into the hot oil, being careful not to overcrowd the pan.
- Fry the boudin balls for 3-4 minutes, or until they are golden brown and crispy on the outside.
- Use a slotted spoon or spider strainer to remove the fried boudin balls from the oil and transfer them to a paper towel-lined plate to drain excess oil. Repeat with the remaining boudin balls.

6. Season and Serve:

- While the boudin balls are still hot, sprinkle them with Creole seasoning (if using) for extra flavor.
- Serve the New Orleans-style Boudin Balls hot, with your favorite dipping sauce on the side.

Enjoy your delicious New Orleans-style Boudin Balls, perfect as an appetizer or party snack!

So why not bring a taste of New Orleans to your next party with these irresistible Boudin Balls? Your guests will thank you for it!

Fried Green Tomatoes

Folks outside of New Orleans, get ready to experience a true taste of the Big Easy with this classic Southern dish - Fried Green Tomatoes. A beloved staple in New Orleans cuisine, these crispy and tangy treats are sure to transport you to the heart of the French Quarter with every bite.

Ingredients:

- 4 medium-sized green tomatoes, sliced into 1/4-inch thick rounds
- 1 cup buttermilk
- 1 cup all-purpose flour
- 1 cup cornmeal
- 1 teaspoon Creole seasoning (or Cajun seasoning)
- 1/2 teaspoon garlic powder
- 1/2 teaspoon paprika
- 1/4 teaspoon cayenne pepper (optional)
- Salt and pepper to taste
- Vegetable oil, for frying
- Remoulade sauce or ranch dressing, for dipping (optional)

Instructions:

1. Prep the Tomatoes:

- Slice the green tomatoes into 1/4-inch thick rounds. Discard the ends.
- Place the tomato slices on a paper towel-lined baking sheet to absorb excess moisture.

2. Soak in Buttermilk:

- In a shallow dish, pour the buttermilk.
- Dip each tomato slice into the buttermilk, coating both sides. Let any excess buttermilk drip off.

3. Prepare the Coating:

In another shallow dish, mix together the all-purpose flour, cornmeal, Creole seasoning, garlic powder, paprika, cayenne pepper (if using), salt, and pepper.

4. Coat the Tomatoes:

Dredge each buttermilk-soaked tomato slice in the flour-cornmeal mixture, ensuring it's well-coated on both sides. Press the coating gently to adhere.

5. Fry the Tomatoes:

- In a large skillet or frying pan, heat vegetable oil over medium-high heat until it reaches about 350°F (175°C).
- Carefully place the coated tomato slices into the hot oil, in batches if necessary to avoid overcrowding the pan.
- Fry the tomatoes for 2-3 minutes on each side, or until they are golden brown and crispy.
- Use a slotted spoon or spatula to transfer the fried green tomatoes to a paper towel-lined plate to drain excess oil. Repeat with the remaining tomato slices.

6. Serve:

Serve the New Orleans-style Fried Green Tomatoes hot, with remoulade sauce or ranch dressing on the side for dipping, if desired.

Enjoy your crispy and flavorful New Orleans-style Fried Green Tomatoes as an appetizer or side dish!

So, whether you're a fan of New Orleans recipes, Cajun cuisine, or just looking to add a touch of Southern flair to your menu, Fried Green Tomatoes are a must-try.

Pecan Pralines

For folks outside New Orleans, the mention of Pecan Pralines might bring to mind a sweet, indulgent treat that is synonymous with the rich culinary traditions of the city. These delectable confections are a staple in New Orleans cuisine, and for good reason – they are absolutely irresistible.

Pecan Pralines

Ingredients:

- 1 cup granulated sugar
- 1 cup packed light brown sugar
- 1/2 cup evaporated milk
- 1/4 cup unsalted butter
- 1 teaspoon vanilla extract
- 1 1/2 cups pecan halves

Instructions:

1. Prepare a Baking Sheet:

Line a baking sheet with parchment paper or wax paper and set aside. This will be used to drop and cool the pralines.

2. Cook the Praline Mixture:

- In a heavy-bottomed saucepan, combine the granulated sugar, brown sugar, evaporated milk, and unsalted butter.
- Cook the mixture over medium heat, stirring constantly, until the sugars dissolve and the mixture comes to a boil.

3. Boil the Mixture:

Once the mixture reaches a boil, reduce the heat to medium-low and continue to cook, stirring occasionally, until a candy thermometer reads 238°F (114°C) or until a small amount of the mixture dropped into cold water forms a soft ball.

4. Add Pecans and Vanilla:

Remove the saucepan from heat and stir in the vanilla extract and pecan halves. Stir until the pecans are evenly coated with the sugar mixture.

5. Drop the Pralines:

Using a spoon or cookie scoop, quickly drop spoonfuls of the praline mixture onto the prepared baking sheet. Work quickly as the mixture will start to set as it cools.

6. Cool and Serve:

- Allow the pralines to cool completely at room temperature until they harden and set, about 30 minutes to 1 hour.
- Once cooled, carefully peel the pralines off the parchment paper and transfer them to an airtight container for storage.

7. Enjoy:

Serve the New Orleans-style Pecan Pralines as a sweet treat or dessert. They make a delicious addition to any holiday table or special occasion.

Enjoy your homemade New Orleans-style Pecan Pralines, packed with sweet, buttery flavor and crunchy pecans!

Pecan Pralines are a wonderful addition to any gathering, whether you are hosting a Mardi Gras party or simply looking to indulge in a taste of New Orleans. These sweet treats are sure to be a hit with anyone who tries them, so be sure to whip up a batch and share them with your loved ones.

So why not bring a taste of New Orleans into your own kitchen with a batch of homemade Pecan Pralines? You'll be glad you did.

Bread Pudding with Whiskey Sauce

If you've never tried bread pudding with whiskey sauce, you're in for a real treat! This classic New Orleans dessert is a must-try for anyone with a sweet tooth. The rich, creamy bread pudding is made with day-old French bread, eggs, sugar, and milk, then baked to perfection. But the real star of the show is the decadent whiskey sauce that is drizzled over the top.

Ingredients:

For the Bread Pudding:

- 6 cups day-old French bread or baguette, torn into small pieces
- 2 cups whole milk
- 4 large eggs
- 1 cup granulated sugar
- 1/4 cup unsalted butter, melted
- 1 teaspoon vanilla extract
- 1 teaspoon ground cinnamon
- 1/4 teaspoon ground nutmeg

- 1/2 cup raisins or dried cranberries (optional)
- 1/2 cup chopped pecans (optional)

For the Whiskey Sauce:

- 1/2 cup unsalted butter
- 1 cup granulated sugar
- 1 large egg
- 1/4 cup whiskey or bourbon
- 1 teaspoon vanilla extract

Instructions:

1. Prepare the Bread Pudding:

- Preheat the oven to 350°F (175°C). Grease a 9x13-inch baking dish with butter or cooking spray.
- Place the torn French bread pieces in the prepared baking dish.

2. Make the Custard Mixture:

- In a large mixing bowl, whisk together the whole milk, eggs, granulated sugar, melted butter, vanilla extract, ground cinnamon, and ground nutmeg until well combined.

- If using, stir in the raisins or dried cranberries and chopped pecans.

3. Pour Over Bread:

Pour the custard mixture over the torn bread pieces in the baking dish. Press down gently to ensure all the bread is soaked in the custard.

4. Bake the Bread Pudding:

Place the baking dish in the preheated oven and bake for 45-50 minutes, or until the bread pudding is set and golden brown on top.

5. Make the Whiskey Sauce:

- While the bread pudding is baking, prepare the whiskey sauce. In a small saucepan, melt the unsalted butter over medium heat.
- Whisk in the granulated sugar and continue to cook, stirring constantly, until the sugar has dissolved.

- In a separate bowl, beat the egg until smooth. Gradually whisk the beaten egg into the sugar mixture, stirring constantly.
- Cook the sauce for 2-3 minutes, or until it thickens slightly.
- Remove the saucepan from heat and stir in the whiskey or bourbon and vanilla extract. Let the sauce cool slightly.

6. Serve:

- Serve the warm bread pudding with a generous drizzle of whiskey sauce over the top.
- Enjoy your delicious New Orleans-style Bread Pudding with Whiskey Sauce as a comforting dessert or sweet treat!

This rich and flavorful dessert is sure to be a hit with family and friends. Enjoy!

So go ahead, channel your inner Creole chef and whip up a batch of this mouthwatering dessert. Your taste buds will thank you, and you'll be transported to the vibrant streets of New Orleans with every bite. Enjoy the flavors of the Big Easy in your own home with this irresistible bread pudding with whiskey sauce recipe.

Chapter 8: Conclusion

Tips for Hosting a New Orleans-Themed Party

If you're looking to bring a taste of New Orleans to your next party, look no further! Hosting a New Orleans-themed party is a fun and festive way to celebrate the vibrant culture and delicious cuisine of the Big Easy. Here are some tips to help you throw a jambalaya jamboree that your guests won't soon forget:

1. Set the scene with some authentic New Orleans decor. Think Mardi Gras beads, fleur-de-lis accents, and colorful masks to give your party that festive flair.

2. Serve up some classic New Orleans dishes like gumbo, jambalaya, and beignets. These iconic dishes are sure to be a hit with your guests and will transport them straight to the streets of the French Quarter.

3. Don't forget the drinks! Whip up a batch of Hurricanes, Sazeracs, or Mint Juleps to keep the party going all night long.

4. Encourage your guests to dress the part by donning their best Mardi Gras attire or Southern-inspired outfits. A little bit of costume fun will add to the festive atmosphere of the party.

5. Keep the party going with some lively New Orleans music. Jazz, blues, and zydeco are all great choices to get your guests up and dancing.

6. Finally, don't forget to indulge in a King Cake for dessert. This traditional Mardi Gras treat is a must-have at any New Orleans-themed party.

By following these tips, you'll be well on your way to hosting a New Orleans-themed party that will have your guests talking about it for years to come. Laissez les bons temps rouler!

Resources for Finding Authentic Ingredients

For folks outside of New Orleans looking to recreate authentic New Orleans recipes, finding the right ingredients can sometimes be a challenge.

However, with the right resources, you can easily locate all the essential components to make delicious dishes like gumbo, jambalaya, beignets, and more.

One of the best places to start your search for authentic ingredients is at your local specialty grocery store. Many stores now carry a wide variety of Cajun and Creole ingredients, such as spices, sauces, and seasonings. Look for brands that are specifically made in Louisiana for the most authentic flavors.

If you can't find what you need at your local grocery store, don't worry! There are plenty of online retailers that specialize in selling New Orleans ingredients. Websites like CajunGrocer.com, LouisianaFoods.com, and NolaCajun.com offer a wide selection of products, from Andouille sausage to file powder to Crystal hot sauce.

For those who prefer to shop in person, consider visiting a local farmers' market or ethnic grocery store.

These places often have unique ingredients that you may not find elsewhere, such as fresh seafood, locally sourced produce, and homemade spice blends.

Lastly, don't forget to reach out to any friends or family members who may have connections to New Orleans. They may be able to recommend specific stores or brands that offer the most authentic ingredients for your recipes.

By utilizing these resources, you can easily find everything you need to make mouthwatering New Orleans dishes right in your own kitchen. So get cooking and enjoy a taste of the Big Easy wherever you are!

Final Thoughts and Well Wishes

To all the folks outside of New Orleans who have embarked on this culinary journey through the vibrant and flavorful world of New Orleans cuisine, we hope you have enjoyed exploring the diverse array of dishes and flavors that make this city a food lover's paradise.

From the spicy Cajun and Creole dishes to the mouthwatering seafood creations, the hearty gumbos and jambalayas, the festive Mardi Gras treats, and the indulgent beignets and po'boys, we hope you have found something to satisfy your cravings and transport you to the bustling streets of the Big Easy.

As you continue to experiment with these recipes in your own kitchen, we encourage you to make them your own by adding your own unique twists and flavors. Don't be afraid to get creative and have fun with the ingredients - after all, that's what New Orleans cuisine is all about!

Whether you're cooking up a pot of gumbo for a cozy night in, frying up some beignets for a special breakfast treat, or baking a king cake for a festive celebration, we hope these recipes bring a little taste of New Orleans into your home and fill your heart with warmth and joy.

So here's to good food, good company, and good times - may your kitchen always be filled with the delicious aromas of New Orleans cuisine, and may your table always be surrounded by laughter and love. Cheers to you, and may your culinary adventures continue to delight and inspire you. Laissez les bons temps rouler - let the good times roll!

www.ingramcontent.com/pod-product-compliance
Lightning Source LLC
Chambersburg PA
CBHW050541160726
48003CB00002B/705